The Little Book of Fine Motor Skills

Helping children to get a grip!

by Sally Featherstone

Illustrations by Kerry Ingham

LITTLE BOOKS WITH BIG IDEAS

First published in the UK by Featherstone Education, 2008
Published 2010 by Featherstone, A&C Black
This edition published 2013 by Featherstone
An imprint of Bloomsbury Publishing Plc
50 Bedford Square, London, WC1B 3DP
www.bloomsbury.com

ISBN 978-1-4081-9412-6

10 9 8 7 6 5 4 3 2 1

A CIP record for this publication is available from the British Library.

Printed in Great Britain by Latimer Trend & Company Limited.

This book is produced using paper that is made from wood grown in
managed, sustainable forests. It is natural, renewable and recyclable.
The logging and manufacturing processes conform to the environmental
regulations of the country of origin.

To see our full range of titles
visit www.bloomsbury.com

Contents

Introduction

Links with the Goals for the Early Years Foundation Stage

This book is one of the titles in a series of Little Books, which explore aspects of practice within the Early Years Foundation Stage in England. The books are also suitable for practitioners working with the early years curriculum in Wales, Northern Ireland and Scotland, and in any early years setting catering for young children.

Across the series you will find titles appropriate to each aspect of the curriculum for children from two to five years, giving practitioners a wealth of ideas for engaging activities, interesting resources and stimulating environments to enrich their work across the Early Years Curriculum.

Each title also has information linking the activity pages to the statutory Early Years curriculum for England. This title has been updated to include the revised Early Learning Goals published by the Department for Education in March 2012.

For the purposes of observation and assessment of the children's work in each activity, we recommend that practitioners should use each of the Revised Statements as a whole, resisting any impulse to separate the elements of each one into short phrases.

The key goals for this title are:

PRIME AREAS

Physical development

①**Moving and handling:** children show good control and co-ordination in large and small movements. They move confidently in a range of ways, safely negotiating space. They handle equipment and tools effectively, including pencils for writing.

SPECIFIC AREAS

Expressive arts and design

①**Exploring and using media and materials:** children sing songs, make music and dance, and experiment with ways of changing them. They safely use and explore a variety of materials, tools and techniques, experimenting with colour, design, texture, form and function.

②**Being imaginative:** children use what they have learnt about media and materials in original ways, thinking about uses and purposes. They represent their own ideas, thoughts and feelings through design and technology, art, music, dance, role-play and stories.

Using this book

Developing control of hands and fingers is a difficult task for most children, and very difficult for some. Many boys are among the group that are less attracted by activities involving the use of fine motor skills, they would far rather be outside, climbing, running, jumping and tumbling, using the strength and gross motor skills they have already mastered.

However, reading, writing, making, constructing and experimenting are all skills that every child needs to learn if they are to have a rich and varied life:

▶ Enjoying and achieving in childhood and beyond

▶ Making a positive contribution to the world around them

▶ Staying safe and healthy, and

▶ Achieving economic well-being

(The Every Child Matters Outcomes)

Play should be at the heart of learning for every child, and the early stages of acquiring any skill should be rooted in playful situations where children are learning through active play and engaging projects, sometimes chosen by the children themselves, and sometimes led by adults.

The growth and development of muscular control in children

Fine motor skills are essential to the future skills of writing, reading and many other key activities in education and in life. These skills develop slowly, and are built on the gross motor skills already established. Control of our muscles develops in a predictable order, and from the core of the body outwards. This starts when babies are born and is not complete until early adulthood.

The 'growth rings' of muscular development

- ▶ The muscles of the neck and core muscles of the trunk develop first, enabling the baby to hold up its own head, and begin to roll over.

- ▶ Next, the back, shoulders and upper arms develop as the baby pushes itself up on its elbows, and begins to be able to sit propped and eventually unaided.

- ▶ Once the upper arms and upper legs have developed (through pulling, pushing and kicking movements), the baby can creep, shuffle and crawl.

- ▶ The refinement of muscles of the shoulder to wrist, and the legs from knee to ankle enable the toddler to stand and begin to move around holding on to people, objects and furniture.

- ▶ Only when the muscles controlling the ankles and feet are ready can toddlers stand unaided and eventually walk. Walking, running, standing, hopping, skipping, riding, kicking, swinging, pulling are all possible now, and toddlers and young children spend hours and hours repeatedly performing, practising and perfecting these skills.

- ▶ Fine motor skills complete their development once the child has control of their hands and fingers, and these skills are among the last to be refined, until the child can, at will, hold, release, catch, throw, play finger games, hold equipment and tools, fix things and take them apart.

The muscle groups can only mature successfully if each stage is built on completed earlier stages of development gained through plenty of practice in play and activity. A missed or incomplete earlier stage will affect a later stage – a child who has not had time to develop shoulder, arm and wrist muscles will not be able to control fine movements of their fingers as easily as a child who has had plenty of unfettered time to play indoors and outside, with toys and equipment appropriate to both their age and their stage of development.

It is no wonder that some children and groups of children make this progress more slowly than others, and these groups may include:

▶ children from environments where movement is restricted by overcrowding, poor housing or anxiety about safety, or where poor diet affects growth;

▶ some boys (who generally develop their fine motor skills later than most girls);

▶ children who have been discouraged from behaving in adventurous or independent ways;

▶ children with delayed or damaged development.

This book will help you to ensure that the development of fine motor skills is built on appropriate early experiences.

Superheroes

Strengthening arms and hands

What you need:

▶ headbands made from strips of stretchy fabric

▶ some 'superhero' music

▶ simple capes made from shiny material tied at the neck

▶ wristbands made from cardboard tubes or hair scrunchies

▶ 'power rings' or 'power sticks' – rubber PE quoits or short lengths of strong cardboard tubes

I will need

Contribution to Early Learning Goals:	
PRIME	**SPECIFIC**
Physical Development ①	Expressive arts & design ① ②

What you do:

This activity will help with concentration as well as strengthening arms, shoulders and hands. The superhero theme will appeal to both boys and girls, especially if you emphasise that everyone can rescue people! Make sure the ground rules are clear before you start (keeping space around you and not touching other children as you work out).

1. Talk with the children about the idea of a workout, and how exercises strengthen their bodies for running, climbing and being superheroes.

2. If you are happy with the costumes, allow the children to wear stretchy headbands or wristbands, but not cloaks, as these may get in the way.

3. Start your workout by doing some warm up exercises – stretching arms in the air, deep breathing, touching toes.

4. Now introduce some specific superhero exercises to strengthen arms and hands. Try these:

   Power punch – punch into the air above your head, out to the sides and in front. Get a rhythm by punching 3 or 4 times in each direction, saying the words 'Punch up high, punch up high; Punch to the side, punch to the side etc.

   Power thrust – with flat hands, thrust up high, to the left and right, in front and down, saying the directions to help them.

   Power stamp – stamping patterns, stamp to the left, one, two, three, four; stamp to the right, one, two, three, four; stamp in a circle one, two, three, four; etc.

5. Children can think up more exercises, but make sure they are solo, not competitive, and always do some gentle relaxing at the end of every session.

And another idea:

▶ Remember that riding bikes, climbing ladders, running and jumping all strengthen children's muscles. Make sure they all (and especially the more active and restless boys) can go out of doors as much as possible to exercise their bodies.

Keep the Beat

Clapping and clicking

What you need:

► most clapping and clicking games need no equipment. However, simple musical instruments such as small drums, tambourines, tabors, chopsticks, short sticks in pairs, cheap plastic bowls or small blocks of wood in pairs can be useful for variety
► a nursery rhyme book

I will need

Contribution to Early Learning Goals:

PRIME
Physical Development ①

SPECIFIC
Expressive arts & design ① ②

What you do:

Accompanying songs, rhymes and other activities by clapping, clicking or playing a steady beat is a very useful way to encourage hand control in an enjoyable way. It costs nothing, needs little preparation and can fill odd times of the day with purpose. Children can clap, stamp, click their fingers, slap their knees or thighs, or play simple homemade or bought percussion instruments. Remember that clicking is much more difficult and some children never really master it – be patient and don't go too fast.

If children are playing instruments, make sure they have something in each hand – this will encourage the use of both sides of the brain as well as concentration and control.

1. Accompany nursery rhymes and simple songs by clapping or clicking.

2. Clap, click and/or stamp as you move from place to place during the day, indoors or outside.

3. Sing or chant language or number songs written for steady beat work, such as 'Keeping the Beat', adding clicking and slapping to the clapping.

4. Clap and click as you count – doing two things at once, and moving while counting helps memory!

5. Play clapping games, and those that involve movements with both sides of the body - such as 'Wind the Bobbin', 'The Hokey Cokey', 'If You're Happy and You Know it', 'Head, Shoulders, Knees and Toes'.

6. Have a birthday or seasonal parade – take an instrument each and march round your setting and outdoor area, singing as you go.

7. Play 'Echo sounds' where the leader claps a short pattern – e.g. clap, click, clap, click – and the children follow. Gradually make the patterns more difficult as children get more confident, and let the children take a turn as leader if they want to.

And another idea:

▶ Put 'clapping games' in Google or another search engine and look for sites that have simple games to suit your children, such as: **www.gameskidsplay.net** or **http://childstoryhour.com**

▶ Buy books of clapping games.

Catch!

Throwing and catching

What you need:

- balls of all sorts and sizes – from footballs to ping-pong balls, soft sponge or plastic
- beanbags
- rubber quoits
- 'koosh' balls
- small soft toys to throw and catch
- small chiffon scarves

Contribution to Early Learning Goals:

PRIME	SPECIFIC
Physical Development ①	Expressive arts & design ① ②

What you do:

Catching is a key skill in hand-eye coordination. Younger children and those with additional needs will require much practice with large soft balls or objects with plenty of texture to catch on to as they develop their skills of seeing, anticipation and grip. Start very close, and praise all their efforts. Here are some ideas:

1. Sit on the floor with one child and roll a soft ball between you. Make sure you start by grabbing their attention – saying 'Look, the ball is coming'. Vary this activity with younger children by using a toy car or other wheeled toy. As they get more practised, in a small group, vary the child you roll the toy to so they must watch all the time!

2. Passing a ball round a small group is another good early activity. Work with three or four children and sit on the floor together. Pass a soft ball that is easy to hold, just going round the group in a predictable order. When children are used to this, you can speed up the passing by clapping along – or you could change the rules by saying 'Change' when the children must start passing in the other direction.

3. As children learn to catch standing up, start with some slow moving objects such as chiffon scarves, balloons or easy to catch objects such as small soft toys, 'koosh' balls, or rolled pairs of socks. Continue to give a signal by saying 'Look, name'.

4. Catching a big ball such as a soft beach ball is good because you can reduce the hardness of the ball for younger children. Stand in a circle with one adult or a child in the middle. The person in the middle chooses who they will throw the ball to, saying the name as they throw. The catcher says the name of the thrower as they throw the ball back.

And another idea:

▶ Sit in two rows and play in pairs with small soft balls or rolled socks.

▶ Have a bucket of beanbags or small balls and throw them one at a time to one or more children who put them in a container.

Good shot!

Aiming

What you need:

- ▶ boxes, baskets, buckets and bowls
- ▶ nets, sheets and other fabrics
- ▶ objects for aiming with – balls, rolled socks, beanbags, sponges
- ▶ water pistols, sprays
- ▶ playground chalk, hoops
- ▶ commercially produced aiming toys such as Velcro targets, aiming games and first dart boards with safe throwing items

Contribution to Early Learning Goals:

PRIME	SPECIFIC
Physical Development ①	Expressive arts & design ① ②

What you do:

Aiming is another way of helping children to coordinate hand and eye. First aiming games can be tossing the toys into their containers at clearing up time, or collecting outdoor equipment to bring indoors. Aiming games and activities are easy to set up, and once you have shown the children the idea, many of them will continue playing on their own or with friends. Introduce aiming activities for kicking as well as throwing. Here are some ideas:

1. Make some soft balls from rolled socks and toss them into a washing-up bowl or bucket.

2. Throw wet sponge balls at a chalk or paint target on a wall or shed, or toss balls into a paddling pool of water.

3. Cut some holes in a sheet or plastic shower curtain. Hang it up indoors or outside and throw objects through the holes.

4. Find or borrow a children's football goal and offer lots of small footballs for goal practice.

5. Buy some arches (or make some from wire coat hangers) and stick them in the grass for a football kicking game or dribbling challenge.

6. Paint a picture on a sheet of plastic or card, fill water pistols or small sprayers and shoot water at the painting until it is washed off.

7. Part fill some plastic water bottles with water or sand, put duct tape round the tops to stop them leaking, and put them on a low wall or table for aiming practice with bean bags.

8. Get a children's basketball hoop and mount it at an easy height on a wall for another sort of aiming.

9. Draw some circles on a sheet and hang it up on a washing line. Use painty sponges, food colouring in water pistols or painty ping-pong balls to make a unique aiming picture.

And another idea:

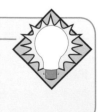

▶ Try **www.tts-group.co.uk** or other educational suppliers for aiming games, targets and other equipment for physical development.

Do it up

Clothes and fastenings

What you need:

- ▶ dressing up clothes with fastenings
- ▶ real babies' and children's clothing and shoes
- ▶ belts, bags and purses with zips and buckles
- ▶ doll's clothes and other toys with fastenings
- ▶ shoes with laces and lacing toys

Contribution to Early Learning Goals:

PRIME	SPECIFIC
Physical Development ①	Expressive arts & design ① ②

What you do:

Learning about fastenings is a key skill for independence, it also gives children opportunities to practise fine motor skills. The use of Velcro and easy fastenings means practitioners have to be inventive in offering children these essential skills. Some ways to do this are:

1. Have real clothes with fasteners in role play areas – real shirts, items with zips and hooks, belts with buckles, bags and purses with zips, laces and clips.

2. Get some life-size baby dolls and provide disposable nappies and real baby clothes for the children to use as they dress and care for the dolls – poppers on babygrows, little buttons etc.

3. Find out if you have any knitters in your community who would be willing to knit some doll's clothes with fastenings like tiny buttons and hooks.

4. Have a shoe or clothes shop role-play with shoes with laces or buckles and clothes with buttons.

5. Make or buy some games or toys that use press studs or laces.

6. Use old shirts with sleeves and collars cut off for overalls – doing the buttons up is great exercise for fingers.

7. Help parents to understand how important it is for children to do up their own clothes and shoes, even if it takes longer. Explain how this sort of activity relates to writing and reading skills. Encourage all children to be independent in these activities as early as possible, and praise their efforts.

8. Make fastenings for boxes and other equipment with little elastic loops and buttons, buckles or tapes to tie.

9. Sew tapes or strings on tents and shelters so children can close them.

And another idea:

▶ Buy some hammer-on press studs from a craft shop and make your own clothes or games, by adding press studs to pieces of stiff card or plastic, or by putting press studs on clothing for dressing up.

Sing-song

Finger play, songs and rhymes

What you need:

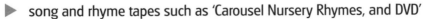

▶ nursery rhyme books with movement rhymes, such as 'This Little Puffin' or 'The Little Book of Nursery Rhymes'
▶ song and rhyme tapes such as 'Carousel Nursery Rhymes, and DVD'
▶ simple props for movement rhymes and songs

I will need

Contribution to Early Learning Goals:

PRIME	SPECIFIC
Physical Development ①	Expressive arts & design ① ②

What you do:

Movement songs and rhymes are a very useful way to encourage concentration and the control of individual fingers needed for writing and other fine motor activities. Here are some favourites and how they help:

1. Insey Winsey Spider – isolating fingers; alternating hands.
2. One finger, one thumb keep moving – isolating parts in sequence.
3. Here are the lady's knives and forks – interlocking fingers.
4. Two little dickey birds – isolating index fingers.
5. Tommy Thumb – isolating individual fingers.
6. Wind the bobbin – hand circling and reversing.
7. Two big fat worms – isolating individual fingers.
8. The wheels on the bus – hand circling.
9. Peter hammers with one hammer – control of individual limbs.
10. We can play on the big bass drum – different ways of using fingers.
11. One, two, three, four, five, once I caught a fish alive – isolating fingers.
12. One potato, two potato – alternating fists.
13. Five fat peas in a pea pod pressed – fist then individual fingers.
14. In a cottage in a wood – hand movements and pointing.
15. Twinkle, twinkle, little star – hand movements.
16. I have ten fingers – isolating individual fingers.
17. Here is a beehive – isolating individual fingers.
18. Open them, shut them – bending and stretching fingers.
19. Little Arabella Miller – 'walking' fingers.
20. Put your finger in the air – pointing.
21. Where is Thumbkin? – isolating individual fingers.

And another idea:

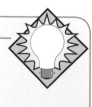

► Put 'action songs', 'finger songs', or 'nursery rhymes' in Google for hundreds of links – **www.kididdles.com** has hundreds of rhymes and songs with the words.

Snip, snap

Cutting and snipping

What you need:

- ▶ good quality scissors of all sorts and sizes
- ▶ leaves, grass, hay, raffia, straw
- ▶ pastry, dough or clay
- ▶ junk mail, magazines, catalogues
- ▶ spaghetti, noodles, tagliatelli
- ▶ salad items such as celery, beans, lettuce

Contribution to Early Learning Goals:	
PRIME	**SPECIFIC**
Physical Development ①	Expressive arts & design ① ②

What you do:

Cutting and snipping are essential skills in controlling both hands in a fine motor activity. Remember that 'cutting out' is a skill that can only develop once children have mastered snipping and cutting straight lines. Some ideas for the snipping and cutting stage are:

1. Offer natural materials such as grass, hay, straw and leaves for snipping. These could be in the garden or brought indoors. Collect fallen leaves on walks and visits for this activity. You could use the snippings for collage work, but the activity is very satisfying in itself.

2. Let children snip the edges of lawns and grassed areas using their own scissors.

3. Cut lots of strips of paper, about (2-3 cm wide) from magazines and junk mail for snipping across into bits.

4. Snip dough and clay 'sausages' or rolled flat pieces, then roll them up for another go.

N.B. Cooking activities using scissors need new or VERY CLEAN scissors.

5. Grate vegetables on a coarse grater and snip the gratings to make soups or carrot cake.

6. Use scissors to snip the margarine into flour for pastry or to chop cherries for buns.

7. Snip herbs such as chives, mint or basil in a cup for flavouring cottage cheese or yogurt dips.

8. Cook some pasta (spaghetti or ribbon types) for just a few minutes and snip them with scissors.

9. Roll out pastry and cut shapes to cook and ice.

10. Snip lettuce, beansprouts or cress to add to sandwiches for snack time, or cut shapes from slices of cucumber.

And another idea:

▶ Make edible 'confetti' from snipped rice paper.

▶ Snip strips of newspaper to make quick papier maché.

▶ Snip strips of thin fabric (stiffened first by painting with thin glue).

Snack time

Spreading and chopping

What you need:

- small plastic and china plates
- children's knives (or butter knives)
- spreads, plates, jams and other fillings
- doilies for presentation
- saucepans and other pots
- small bowls for mixing
- small forks

Contribution to Early Learning Goals:	
PRIME	**SPECIFIC**
Physical Development ①	Expressive arts & design ① ②

What you do:

Preparing their own food, and food for others, gives children a huge sense of achievement. Make sure children get the opportunity to do this regularly as part of healthy eating and snack programmes. Of course, you need to make sure the cutlery for these activities is clean and kept just for food preparation and CHECK FOR FOOD ALLERGIES. Some ideas are:

1. Toast bread, bagels, crumpets or muffins, and let children spread their own and cut them into fingers or shapes.

2. Help the children to make some simple dips from yogurt or cream cheese to spread on small savoury biscuits or rice cakes.

3. Let the children slice some pitta breads and use these to dip into homemade humus (mix a tin of chick peas with a little oil, some garlic and some salt and mash with a spoon).

4. Hard boil some eggs and let the children chop them finely to mix with a little mayonnaise for sandwiches.

5. Make cheese straws.

6. Offer some different fillings, so children can make their own sandwiches from sliced bread.

7. Get some cheap vegetables such as carrots, parsnips, cabbage and let the children practise chopping in the home area before making the chopped vegetables into soup or stew.

8. Chop apples for a home-made apple pie, or pears to make a tart. Or make uncooked 'instant jam' by chopping strawberries or raspberries finely and mixing with a little sugar. Leave for an hour before eating. Keeps for up to three days in a fridge.

9. Cut celery and carrots into short pieces for the children to cut into sticks for vegetable dips or salsa.

And another idea:

▶ Make some pancakes and spread them with jam, chocolate spread or savoury dip, roll them up to eat.

▶ Squeeze honey from the plastic sort of bottles, and spread on warm toast.

Fringe

Fringing and folding

What you need:

- ▶ card, strong paper, magazine pages, junk mail
- ▶ thin fabric and thin glue to make stiffened fabric shapes for snipping
- ▶ foil cases
- ▶ paper cases for buns, muffins and cakes
- ▶ crêpe paper, foil paper
- ▶ clean plastic packaging from chocolates, cakes and buns

Contribution to Early Learning Goals:

PRIME	SPECIFIC
Physical Development ①	Expressive arts & design ① ②

What you do:

Another scissor activity that helps fine motor skills is fringing. Add folding to the children's repertoire of methods and they will be able to embark on many different creative activities, often unsupervised. Here are some:

1. Practise fringing by offering shapes of card, strong paper and fabric (stiffened by painting with thin glue and drying) for children to fringe all the way round. This is an activity in itself and doesn't need to be made into a product.

2. Make simple puppets from paper plates on the end of sticks. Paint a face and use fringed paper for hair.

3. Make fringes for the edges of display boards.

4. Fringe strips of green paper, roll them up, stick the end, then gently pull the middle out to make little trees.

5. Get some decorated or coloured paper bun cases, and fringe them to make flowers. Add a little circle of yellow paper for the centre, and stick on the end of flattened straws.

6. Make party wigs by fringing foil paper and sticking the edge to a headband.

7. Make hula skirts by fringing crêpe paper and sticking or stapling to a waist tape.

8. Make paper lanterns by folding a strip of paper in half lengthways and snipping from the fold, almost to the edge. Unfold, curl round and stick or staple the ends.

9. Make stars by fringing the edges of foil trays from jam tarts or plastic trays from chocolates.

10. Make streamers by fringing crêpe paper strips and twisting them as you hang them up.

And another idea:

▶ Learn about more complex fringing activities by exploring 'quilling'.

▶ Let children incorporate their folding and fringing skills when they make masks, hats and other festive objects.

A necklace for you

Threading

What you need:

- ▶ beads (wooden, plastic, paper), dry pasta tubes, card tubes, plastic straws
- ▶ laces (with stiffened ends), string, treasury tags, wool, raffia, cord
- ▶ sorting trays for sorting beads

I will need

Contribution to Early Learning Goals:	
PRIME	**SPECIFIC**
Physical Development ①	Expressive arts & design ① ②

What you do:

Threading is a familiar activity in many early years settings. It is a clean, easy, independent activity that helps children with fine motor control. Add some of these ideas to your list of ways to make and use these simple resources.

1. Colour some uncooked pasta tubes and 'elbow' shapes by putting them in a zip-lock bag with a few drops of food colouring. Massage the bag until the pasta is coloured, and tip out to dry before using.

2. Cut some thin slices of apple and orange and dry them in the oven for festive threading. Or thread popcorn using a thick darning needle threaded with red wool or cotton.

3. Make some simple repeating pattern cards for children to copy as they thread and make necklaces.

4. Offer the children some thin elastic for threading beads for bracelets and wristbands for superheroes.

5. Get a bargain pack of plastic straws and let the children snip them into their own beads for threading. You could even make them into a 'bead curtain'.

6. Make your own shoelaces by dipping the end of cord or string in PVA glue and hanging up to dry.

7. Make perfumed rose beads. Collect petals with the children. Put them in a food processor (adult only) and whizz until you have a paste. Scoop up a bit of the paste and roll it into a ball the size of a big pea. Put a cocktail stick through the middle and poke the stick into a ball of dough or clay to dry. When dry, thread the perfumed beads on thin string.

8. Show the children how to use a hole punch and let them punch holes in card and join bits with string or treasury tags.

And another idea:

▶ Make your own paper beads. Wind narrow strips of pasted paper round a paper or plastic drinking straw. Leave to dry, then snip the straw at the end of each bead. This makes threading much easier.

Go fish!

Fishing games

What you need:

- ▶ magnets, magnet tape
- ▶ string and wool
- ▶ paper and thin plastic (from tough carrier bags)
- ▶ paper clips
- ▶ washers, small toys, sequins, ring pulls
- ▶ small sieves, nets, tea strainers
- ▶ green garden sticks or short bamboo canes for fishing rods

Contribution to Early Learning Goals:

PRIME	SPECIFIC
Physical Development ①	Expressive arts & design ① ②

What you do:

Fishing games take great concentration and dexterity as the rod and line are at a distance from the eyes and hands. Be patient with these sorts of games, and start with easy fishing where children use nets instead of rods.

1. Use a paddling pool or baby bath outside and float ducks or plastic fish in coloured water. Let the children fish with small sieves, tea strainers or children's fishing nets (cut the handles down if they are dangerously long). You could put numbers on for scoring, but counting the objects is enough for most children.

2. Make a fishing game in an aquarium of water. Use sequins, beads, small toys, and try to make sure that some of the objects float, some sink, and some float just below the surface. The children can fish with tea strainers or small sieves.

3. Make a first magnet game with small magnets tied to strings (with no fishing rods) and let children fish in water or dry tanks for plastic or paper fish with paper clips fixed to their heads. Card fish may be too heavy to lift, so check your magnets are strong enough.

4. When children have mastered the easier games, make a game with fishing rods, strings and magnets. This is easier in a dry tank.

5. A real challenge for some children is to put an opened paper clip on the end of the fishing string and let them try picking up 'ring pulls' from drinks cans (these won't work with magnets!).

6. Have a competition to see who can make the longest string of paper clips on the end of their magnet.

7. Use some small world worms or snakes for a different fishing game. You could put numbers on the snakes to make it a mathematical scoring game.

And another idea:

▶ Horseshoe or ring magnets are easiest to tie on strings, but you could use button magnets mounted on card, and cut round the card leaving a border that you can punch a hole through for the string.

Careful!

Drippers and droppers

What you need:

- plastic pipettes, droppers and syringes
- food colouring (get big quantities at reasonable prices from TTS – **www.tts-group.co.uk**)
- plastic beakers and other transparent containers

Contribution to Early Learning Goals:

PRIME	SPECIFIC
Physical Development ①	Expressive arts & design ① ②

What you do:

Droppers, pipettes, syringes and other sorts of tubes help children to control their fine movements while they explore objects and substances. Food colouring and thin paint are ideal solutions to offer for this sort of work.

1. Offer droppers and different colours of paint or food colouring with dry paper or fabric, on a flat surface as a first experience. When children have mastered using the droppers and pipettes, let them experiment with wet paper, blotting paper, paper tissues, kitchen roll and different sorts of fabrics.

2. Offer droppers and concentrated food colouring to add a new dimension to shaving foam or gloop (cornflour and water).

3. Collect some clear plastic containers and experiment with adding very small amounts of colouring to water and watching what happens as it mixes with the water. A plastic aquarium is great for this activity.

4. Put a long strip of paper on a slide or a sloped plank and have drip races from the top, using droppers and pipettes with runny paint or coloured water.

5. Put paper on the floor indoors or outside and make big drip patterns and pictures as a group. Black paper and fluorescent colours can be very effective.

6. Transfer coloured water between very small containers using droppers, syringes and pipettes.

7. Make jewel patterns by dropping coloured drops of water from droppers onto the suckers on a soap saver (look at 'soap saver' on Google images if you don't know what this is). Take prints of these on blotting paper or kitchen paper.

8. Float a piece of paper on water and drop colours on to it until it sinks!

And another idea:

▶ Get pipettes, syringes and droppers from **www.commotionstore.co.uk** which has bargain prices for bulk purchases!

Tweeze it

Tweezers and tongs

What you need:

- ▶ plastic tweezers – get good value medical ones from **www.stjohnsupplies.co.uk**
- ▶ kitchen tongs of all sorts
- ▶ bamboo tongs
- ▶ salad tongs
- ▶ small objects to pick up – pasta shapes, sequins, small beads, rice, malleable materials

Contribution to Early Learning Goals:	
PRIME	**SPECIFIC**
Physical Development **①**	Expressive arts & design **① ②**

What you do:

Tweezers and tongs are great for developing concentration, grip and control. Get as many different sorts as you can (pound shops and kitchen stores are great places) and use them for all sorts of activities. Here are a few to add to your stock:

1. Use plastic first aid tweezers to pick up small objects such as sequins, small beads, lentils, pasta stars, little buttons. Offer children sorting trays or ice cube trays to sort into.

2. Put some plastic balls in a bucket of paint and use tongs to pick the painty balls up and drop them into a paddling pool lined with paper. This makes an interesting picture.

3. Use tweezers to pick up strands of cooked pasta (add a couple of drops of oil to the pasta to stop it sticking together). You could colour the pasta several colours and challenge children to sort it out on to plates, taking a colour each.

4. Have fun eating baked beans with tweezers or chopsticks!

5. Catch strands of plastic cut from plastic carrier bags, which are floating in coloured water.

6. Use tweezers to pick small items from a pile of gloop (cornflour and water) or foam, or from a sand tray.

7. Paint a piece of card with white glue and use tweezers to drop small beads and sequins on the glue to make a picture or pattern.

8. Get some of the 'holes' from hole punches and have a competition to see who can pick up most in one go – counting them is great fun!

9. Use tweezers or small tongs to pinch bits of clay or dough and lift them into toy trucks.

10. Lift grains of rice into numbered sorting trays for tiny counting.

And another idea:

▶ Cook some spaghetti and provide each child with a plastic water bottle and a pair of tweezers. The challenge is to get as much of the spaghetti in their bottle as they can. Vary the game by colouring some of the spaghetti.

Very small

Tiny drawings

What you need:

- ▶ cotton buds, toothpicks, cocktail sticks, feathers
- ▶ small pieces of card, paper, polystyrene, foil card, flat plastic from clean food containers
- ▶ PVA glue and paint

Contribution to Early Learning Goals:

PRIME	SPECIFIC
Physical Development ①	Expressive arts & design ① ②

What you do:

Very small things fascinate many children, and this can be encouraged by offering activities on a small scale. Painting and mark-making can be very absorbing to children. Here are some ideas:

1. Roll out some clay into small rectangles and use cocktail sticks or small twigs from the garden to make pictures by scratching and poking the surface. Make these into interesting structures by curving them into cylinders or bridge shapes.

2. Spread foam or gloop on a table or board, adding some colour if you like, and offer cotton buds to make patterns and marks in the foam.

3. On damp days make little pictures in the mud outside, using sticks or old pencils.

4. Mix PVA glue with paint, and make pictures on small pieces of card or other surfaces with cotton buds or feathers. Make these little paintings into mobiles by suspending them on cotton from coat hangers or a washing line.

5. Get some old cups, plates and other plain items from a charity shop or rummage sale and decorate these with patterns of paint, using small brushes and cotton buds.

6. Collect some plastic plant pots and decorate them using the tiny tools. Add little decorations such as sequins and small beads – picking them up by putting a toothpick through the hole.

7. Colour small pieces of card with bright coloured crayons. Cover the bright colours with black crayon and then scratch through with a toothpick. This is really fine work, and some children may rather use a sharp pencil to scratch through the black to reveal the colours.

8. Paint on an unbreakable mirror with paint, then wash it off again.

And another idea:

▶ Always offer different sized pieces of paper and a range of sizes of mark making tools. Some children love writing tiny letters and making tiny cards and books to send to their friends and families.

Get messy!

Water, mud and paint

What you need:

▶ child-sized brooms, trowels and other garden tools.
   Try **www.plantmenow.co.uk**, **www.garden-gear.co.uk** or
   www.qualitygardentools.com

▶ buckets and bowls

▶ brushes of all sizes

▶ builders' or cement mixing trays

▶ a hose

Always wash hands after using mud.

Contribution to Early Learning Goals:

PRIME	SPECIFIC
Physical Development ①	Expressive arts & design ① ②

What you do:

Water and mud must have been among the first mark making materials used by humans. Children are still fascinated by them, so make the most of it and build these free resources into your activities for developing fine motor skills by offering some of the following:

1. Digging in a special digging patch in the garden is a real treat for many children – they don't want to be gardeners, just diggers! Provide child-sized garden tools and buckets, and just let them play. The activity will strengthen arms, shoulders and hands in preparation and to support fine motor control.

2. Offer children buckets of water and brushes so they can make muddy water to paint on paths and walls (or paper pinned to fences). A hose for washing the mud away is another way to use physical skills, concentration, and develop a sense of responsibility. An outside tap is a fantastic resource for everyone.

3. Collect plastic plant pots of all sizes and let the children use them to fill and empty and make mud pies. If you haven't got a garden, offer some compost in a builder's tray.

4. Put some wet mud or compost in a builder's tray and use toy cars and trucks to make tracks in the mud.

5. Ride trikes and drive cars through puddles and watch the tracks the wet wheels make.

6. Get some child-sized brooms and sweep the water from puddles on wet days, or use chalk on paths and patios and use wet brushes to wash the chalk away.

7. Use sticks or old paint brushes to make patterns and pictures in muddy puddles.

And another idea:

▶ When you go out, make sure the children have suitable footwear and feel free to walk in leaves, mud and puddles. Play 'Poohsticks' by racing twigs under bridges. Investigate the way mud behaves in different weathers and seasons.

Get sticking!

Sticky tape

What you need:

▶ all sorts of tapes – see opposite

▶ good quality scissors and dispensers

▶ a range of clean recycled materials such as boxes, cartons, tubes, cones, plastic trays, pots, tubs, egg boxes

▶ opportunities to work on a larger scale with big cartons such as those from household goods

---

Contribution to Early Learning Goals:

PRIME	SPECIFIC
Physical Development ①	Expressive arts & design ① ②

What you do:

Sticky tape is fascinating and very helpful in strengthening hands and fingers. Use tapes that children can manage themselves, and show them how to use them.

Make sure your construction and creative areas have plenty of tapes of different sorts. Look in pound shops, or buy in bulk to get good prices that will allow free access for children who need lots of tape for projects. Once they have plenty of tapes and permission to use them, children just need a range of recycled materials and time to work. Try some of these sorts of tape:

1. Masking tape – the easiest tape for children to use, as children can tear it without any help.

2. Transparent sellotape – often very cheap in big rolls from bargain shops. Provide dispensers and teach children about the sharp cutters on them.

3. Silver duct tape – thicker, and harder to tear, but very satisfying because it will stick most things and is waterproof. Children may appreciate having some strips torn for them and attached somewhere handy until they get the hang of tearing it across the roll.

4. Brown parcel tape – this is very cheap, but thin and needs care because it often gets stuck to itself. You could get a tape gun for adult use when children ask for help with big projects (they are too difficult and sharp for children to use).

5. Double sided tape – great for most surfaces, but more expensive.

6. Hook and Loop (Velcro) tape and patches – these stick to most surfaces and are good for any project where you want to attach and detach parts.

And another idea:

▶   Make sure you have somewhere to store unfinished models and creations. Children really need to be able to return to projects over time, if they are to develop concentration and focus on their work.

Tie it up

String, wool and tying

What you need:

- all sorts of string, ribbon, cotton, wool, thread, rope in long and shorter lengths
- good quality scissors
- plastic or plastic covered fencing
- trellis
- hooks, clips, elastic bands

I will need

Contribution to Early Learning Goals:

PRIME	SPECIFIC
Physical Development ①	Expressive arts & design ① ②

What you do:

Fixing, tying and stringing items are all essential skills in training muscles for writing, technology and construction. They also give children opportunities to solve simple problems and adjust their work to achieve a successful outcome. Tying and fixing needs concentration as well as skill – here are some ideas:

1. Collect a range of materials for tying and fixing objects – string, cotton, wool, rope, raffia, ribbon, garden twine, fabric tape, soft wire.

2. Use fences and railings as bases for tying and fixing objects of all sorts. Tying up your trike to stop it rolling away, fixing a waterway to the fence so it can work, tying a big hook or pulley to the climbing frame for lifting, fixing fabric to the underside of a platform to make a house. These are all good reasons to find and learn how to use strings and other fixings.

3. If you haven't got a fence, buy some garden fencing or trellis for tying things to, or hang natural or found objects from bushes and trees.

4. Challenge the children to find or bring objects with holes and hang them from a fence or other structure to make a hanging sculpture – washers, ring pulls, tubes, stones with holes – see what they can find over a week, and photograph the ways they devise for hanging them up.

5. Offer some balls of string for tying and constructing string patterns around your garden.

6. Get the sort of elastics you can use for roof racks and explain how to use them safely.

7. Find other objects that can be tied to strings to help suspend pictures, paintings, models or mobiles. Try bulldog clips, clothes pegs, small hooks, ring magnets etc.

And another idea:

▶ Help children manage balls of string by putting the ball in a plastic box with a lid. Make a hole in the lid and thread the end of the string through the hole, so the children can pull out the length they need.

And so to sew

Weaving and sewing

What you need:

▶ different sorts of knitting wool, including those with bobbles and unusual textures (buy odd balls from craft shops)

▶ card, boxes, string for looms

▶ feathers and other natural objects

▶ darning needles or sewing needles for children

▶ fabric glue

Contribution to Early Learning Goals:

PRIME	SPECIFIC
Physical Development ①	Expressive arts & design ① ②

What you do:

Sewing and weaving can either be a whole body activity or a contemplative, quiet occupation. Whichever way children choose, these activities will involve them in using their fingers and hands to manage threads, fabrics and other soft materials to create structures and objects. Here are just a few ideas:

1. A traditional sewing activity in education is the use of big needles and a sort of canvas called 'Binca'. The canvas has regular holes which make it easy for young children to push a needle and coloured thread through to make patterns. Some children love this, others find it very frustrating, but you could offer some for them to try.

2. Try paper weaving, with strips of strong paper – See the Little Book of Sewing and Weaving for lots of ideas and instructions.

3. Show children how to wind wool, string or narrow strips of fabric round short sticks or other natural objects to make binding sculptures.

4. Collect some fruit and vegetable nets or even potato sacks made from loose weave fabric and cut these into pieces to use with big needles and wool or thin coloured string.

5. Buy or make some simple weaving frames. Use shoe box lids and wind string round to make a loom which children can weave into with wool or narrow strips of fabric. Or make some card looms by cutting notches in rectangles of strong card from packaging boxes. Wind string round between the notches and weave between the strings.

6. Use two lolly sticks tied together in a cross as a very easy frame for weaving. Google 'God's Eye Weaving' to see some examples.

7. Offer some feathers, leaves, grasses and flowers for children to add to their weavings to make them more complex and interesting.

And another idea:

▶ Find some great weaving resources at Mindstretchers
   www.mindstretchers.co.uk

▶ Look at the Montessori weaving pages at
   www.montessoriworld.org/Handwork/weave/weaving1.html

Waving

Ribbons, scarves and flags

What you need:

- ▶ scarves of all sorts, including chiffon, silk, cotton
- ▶ fabric remnants, old sheets and pillowcases
- ▶ cotton tape, ribbon
- ▶ lightweight string
- ▶ carrier bags
- ▶ short sticks, canes, chopsticks

Contribution to Early Learning Goals:

PRIME
Physical Development ①

SPECIFIC
Expressive arts & design ① ②

What you do:

Ribbons, flags and scarves are all good resources to improve movement skills – they can be used to strengthen shoulder and arm muscles as well as precise hand and finger movements. Use for adult-directed and child-initiated activities such as:

1. Get some small chiffon scarves to use for simple catching and waving games. You can also use these for practising letter formation in a gross motor way, as children use their shoulders and arms to make huge letters in the air.

2. Buy or make some ribbon sticks. Homemade ones are just ribbons tied to the ends of short sticks such as chopsticks or green garden sticks. Use these for free play out of doors or for more controlled movements in big spaces indoors.

3. Cut or tear fabric into squares and triangles to make flags of all sizes. Old pillow cases are useful, as each one makes two big flags that children can decorate and attach to canes for parades. Cut or tear a range of different scraps of fabric into small triangles and staple to cotton tape to make bunting to decorate your garden for a special occasion. Tie your flags to climbing frames, fences and sheds, and make special flags for castle, pirate, or story play.

4. Make instant, cheap kites from plastic carrier bags – slit the bottom and tie the handles to a piece of thin string. Decorate them if you like, with paint mixed with PVA glue, then run in the wind and fly them.

5. Visit a charity shop and buy some big square silky scarves. These make superb parachutes for parachute play with small groups.

6. Use squares of thin fabric or fabric handkerchiefs to make parachutes for puppets, soft toys or superhero figures.

And another idea:

▶ If you can afford to buy ribbon sticks, try to get ones with swivels on the ends – these make the ribbons move in a different and more creative way. Try **www.spacekraft.co.uk** for sets of these.

Stretchy

Lycra and elastic

What you need:

► stretchy fabrics
► squares and strips of lycra (you can get lycra from dance shops and fabric stalls)
► soft toys, beach balls and balloons

I will need

Contribution to Early Learning Goals:	
PRIME	**SPECIFIC**
Physical Development ①	Expressive arts & design ① ②

What you do:

Stretchy fabrics and objects give children experience of tension and something to push against as they develop their muscles and test their strength. Some ideas for using lycra and other stretchy materials are:

1. Use squares of lycra (or other stretchy materials) for games where children test their strength by pulling against the edges and bouncing objects on the surface.

2. Use the lycra to encourage cooperative play with small groups. Bounce objects and toys – balloons, beach balls, soft toys or puppets by working together to keep the lycra stretched.

3. Some children with coordination difficulties may like to be wrapped in a piece of lycra and held gently so they can push against the fabric. **Don't do this with any child who shows distress, only the ones who enjoy it!** You could also make some stretchy suits by sewing up lycra into a rectangular bag, big enough for a child to wear, with just their head sticking out of a hole at the top, and their hands and feet in the corners, as they punch and push against the stretchy material.

4. Use some strips of lycra, tied or sewn together to make a big stretchy band that a single child or a small group can use together for 'stretchy' trust and tension activities. Sit in a group and put the stretchy band behind you so you can all lean against the band and support each other. Smaller versions of these bands (sometimes used for pilates) can be used by individual children to stretch between their shoulders and feet, or hands and feet as they sit on the floor.

And another idea:

▶ Look at and buy bands called Trust/resistance bands from TTS **www.tts-group.co.uk**

▶ Stretchy, knitted fabrics of any sort can be used for these activities – they don't fray, so they don't need hemming!

Build it

Tree ties, cable ties, bag fasteners

What you need:

- ▶ tree, plant, cable, plastic bag and other plastic ties
- ▶ good quality scissors
- ▶ canes and sticks
- ▶ big pieces of fabric and card
- ▶ lightweight fabric or plastic sheet to cover constructions
- ▶ clothes pegs and other clips

Contribution to Early Learning Goals:

PRIME	SPECIFIC
Physical Development ①	Expressive arts & design ① ②

What you do:

Packets of ties for garden, DIY and household use are instant and fascinating resources for children, especially for large scale construction. They are cheap (try bargain shops and DIY superstores for big packs). Show the children how to use them, then offer these alongside other fastenings when children are working independently outside as well as indoors. Some ideas:

1. Offer tree and cable ties with canes or other sticks to make dens and shelters indoors and outside. When the children have finished their construction, they can cover it with lightweight fabric, fixed with clothes pegs.

2. Make smaller constructions for soft toys and small world figures by using cable ties to fasten green garden canes.

3. Use the ties to fix fabric to fences, climbing frames and other vertical surfaces by making small holes in the fabric and using ties to fix it to the structure.

4. Fix shower curtains or big sheets of card from very big cartons to pipes and other uprights to make painting or drawing surfaces. Make small holes with a pencil or a stick and thread the ties through. Join them together to make a longer tie. Children may need to be shown how to do this.

5. Add plastic bag ties to construction materials for fixing all sorts of things together.

6. Use plant ties to support plants such as beans and sunflowers as they grow up sticks and strings.

7. Connect ties to each other in a chain to make a decorative support for a hanging plant or a mobile.

8. Remember ties need cutting with scissors to remove them!

And another idea:

▶ Use the internet to find real bargains at wholesale prices.

Spray it on

Pouring and spraying

What you need:

- ▶ spray bottles – new or recycled (make sure recycled bottles are clean)
- ▶ food colouring or thin paint
- ▶ shower curtains, old sheets
- ▶ jugs to fill the spray bottles

Contribution to Early Learning Goals:

PRIME	SPECIFIC
Physical Development ①	Expressive arts & design ① ②

What you do:

If you get some small hand sprays – the sort for spraying house plants, the children can have some fun while they strengthen their grip and improve the separation of their index fingers by squeezing the triggers. Water pistols use just the same muscles, so you may want to add some of these too!

1. When you first offer these sprays, children just need to play with them, so fill them with water for spraying on windows or other surfaces outside.

2. Use the sprays to spray water on plants and trees, or just on the ground. If you do this on a hot day the children will be fascinated with the way the water disappears. Use this as a talking point and for some shared thinking.

3. Hang up a shower curtain, an old sheet or some huge pieces of paper out of doors, and mix some food colouring and water to put in the sprays. You may or may not need to agree some rules for use of the sprays, it depends on you and the children.

4. When the children have had plenty of time to explore the coloured sprays and what they can do, try just spraying at the top of the paper and watching the dribbles run. Use the sprays to spray colour on to damp sheets of paper laid flat on a table or the floor.

5. Try contrast spraying by using white paint on black paper, black paint on red paper, or themed colours of paint to make lovely backing paper for seasonal or themed displays.

6. Spray cellulose paste and sprinkle glitter on it before it dries.

7. Paint some targets, objects or faces on an old sheet and use the sprays or water pistols to aim at the targets.

8. Float some plastic ducks in a paddling pool and spray them to make them move across the pool.

And another idea:

▶ There are all sorts of spray bottles, try to get a range.

▶ If you are re-using bottles, make very sure they are absolutely clean before the children use them. Even plant food or cosmetics should be completely removed.

Make a cake

Icing and decorating

What you need:

- icing sugar
- food colouring
- icing pens
- food colouring pens
- tweezers
- foil or greaseproof paper
- small decorations – hundreds and thousands, chocolate and coloured sprinkles, icing flowers

---

Contribution to Early Learning Goals:

PRIME	SPECIFIC
Physical Development ①	Expressive arts & design ① ②

What you do:

This activity, which is really writing and drawing, can be done on biscuits and buns you have made yourselves, or ones you have bought. Here are some ideas for things to do:

1. Let each child put their own bun or biscuit on a small square of foil or greaseproof paper, it will be easier to move when they have finished.

2. Help the children to make some simple icing with icing sugar and water, divide it into small bowls, and colour each with a different food colouring. Let the children choose how they will ice their buns or biscuits, using just a teaspoon to spoon and drizzle the icing. You could offer coloured sprinkles, hundreds and thousands or chocolate strands to decorate the icing if you like.

3. Once children have got the knack of how icing behaves, show them how to spoon a bigger blob of icing on the bun or biscuit so it covers the whole of the top, then use icing pens to draw, make patterns or blobs, or write on top in a different colour.

4. Make bought fairy cakes into butterfly cakes by helping the children to cut the top off, spread the bun with butter icing, and then cut the top in half to make butterfly wings. (Google 'butterfly cakes' to see what they should look like.)

5. Ice savoury biscuits with cream cheese. You can buy cream cheese in tubes so children can make patterns, then decorate the biscuits with chopped chives, tiny bits of tomato or peas. These could be picked up with tweezers!

6. Older children can plan their icing and decorations before they start.

And another idea:

▶ Look in bargain shops for cheap icing sets with plunger tubes to fill with your own icing. You could use these to write on paper with paint or flour and water mixture, but don't use them for food afterwards!

See it through

Tracing

What you need:

- ▶ tracing paper (or greaseproof paper, which is cheaper)
- ▶ soft pencils, felt pens
- ▶ comics and children's magazines
- ▶ simple clip art
- ▶ cooking oil and cotton balls
- ▶ paper clips
- ▶ cellophane

I will need

Contribution to Early Learning Goals:

PRIME	SPECIFIC
Physical Development ①	Expressive arts & design ① ②

What you do:

Tracing is another traditional hand-eye coordination activity that children have been doing for years. Tracing names and simple black line pictures are both good for this sort of training. Here are some more ideas:

1. Trace over pictures in children's magazines and comics, and use the tracings to make pictures or new stories. Boys may well be more motivated by tracing superheroes or cars!

2. Use simple clip art to make tracing pictures, then challenge the children to trace funny composite pictures such as 'a postman with a cup on his head', 'a bird eating a banana', 'Superman standing on a chimney', 'a big spider near a very small boy'. The inventiveness of this activity will depend on the variety of the clip art you provide!

3. Offer the children simple shape patterns to trace, then colour these with felt pens. When they are finished, gently cover the back of the picture with a little cooking oil on a cotton ball. This will make the colours in the tracings glow, especially if you stick them to a window.

4. Use children's own drawings for tracing practice. Give them black felt pens to draw with and then either photocopy or scan the drawings to make tracing cards for other children to use.

5. Try tracing on coloured cellophane using permanent marker pens. Make sure the children can see through the cellophane.

6. Show older children how to make a transfer from their tracing. Trace a simple picture using a soft pencil. Then turn the tracing over onto a clean sheet of paper and trace the back of the tracing lines. This will transfer the picture to the new piece of paper. Put the two pictures and the original together and talk about what you see and why this has happened.

And another idea:

▶ Explore carbon paper. Make sure the paper and carbon paper are firmly clipped together. Or use carbonated duplicate pads. Children will love this magic way of writing or drawing.

Sort it out

Sorting small objects

What you need:

▶ ice cube trays and other trays with small sections for sorting

▶ plastic tweezers

▶ small spoons

▶ small and very small items to sort – these can be bought (sequins, beads, pasta shapes, rice, dried beans) or found (buttons, shells, pumpkin or melon seeds etc)

I will need

Contribution to Early Learning Goals:	
PRIME	**SPECIFIC**
Physical Development ①	Expressive arts & design ① ②

What you do:

Many children love sorting interesting objects and will spend long periods of time exploring boxes of bits and pieces. Collect some very small objects for sorting with fingers or tweezers to encourage hand-eye coordination and concentration. Provide sorting trays, bun trays or ice cube trays for these little sorting activities. Remember, this is NOT a punishment! – Keep the quantities small enough for it to be a rewarding activity. For some children 20 objects will be enough. Some ideas for tiny sorting are:

1. Get a bag of small mixed beads from a craft shop. Tip them into a bowl and let the children sort them in any way they wish – by colour, shape, size etc.

2. Find some celebration sequin shapes and mix two or three different shapes, e.g. pumpkins and bats; stars and moons; balloons and bows; holly leaves and candles; numbers. Offer tweezers to use for sorting if they want them.

3. Mix lentils, dried sweetcorn kernels, pasta stars, dried red adzuki beans and green flageolet beans for sorting with fingers.

4. Collect some small buttons (from charity shops or the spare buttons provided in clothing) and sort these by colour, type, number of holes, garment type etc.

5. Buy a box of coloured paper clips and make a chain of each colour.

6. Collect small screws, washers and nuts for sorting.

7. Colour some rice grains by shaking them up in a zip-lock bag with a few drops of food colouring. Dry them before mixing the colours for a dedicated sorter to sort into an ice cube tray.

And another idea:

▶ Buy a plastic box with lots of compartments and collect small, interesting objects to fill it for children to explore. Or give children a selection of small boxes for collecting small treasures to examine, share and sort.

Snail trails

Salt pots and trails

What you need:

▶ tough glass or plastic containers such as salt pots, deodorant bottles, plastic sauce and ketchup bottles, washing-up liquid bottles

▶ paint, salt, flour

▶ straws and brushes

I will need

Contribution to Early Learning Goals:

PRIME
Physical Development ①

SPECIFIC
Expressive arts & design ① ②

What you do:

These activities need control and hand-eye coordination, but they are also very enjoyable for children to do. Drizzling powder or liquids on all sorts of surfaces from all sorts of heights will result in some very ingenious work. Here are some ideas:

1. Colour some sand by mixing it with powder or liquid paint and leaving it in a warm place to dry. Put the coloured sand in salt pots for drizzling in shallow trays. If you cover the paper with glue first, the sand will stick. You can use glitter or salt too – salt makes sparkly patterns on black paper.

2. Mix some thin paint with self-raising flour for 'Puffy Paint'. Pour it into clean washing-up liquid bottles. Use this to make patterns and trails. The paint will puff up as it dries, due to the raising agent in the flour. Adding some salt will make the paint glisten when it dries.

3. Put some big sheets of paper on the ground outside. Let children drizzle runny paint from straws and brushes to make a big picture.

4. Fill washing-up liquid bottles with water for making wet trails around the garden.

5. Fill a washing-up bottle half full with paint and put the cap firmly on. Hang the bottle upside-down over a big piece of paper. Carefully remove the cap and gently swing the bottle over the paper. Watch what happens!

6. Try dipping string or rope in paint or water and using it to make trails on paper or on the ground outside.

7. Use salt pots filled with paint to write letters and names on paper.

8. Fill ball roller deodorant bottles with paint and use these for writing and drawing.

And another idea:

▶ Bargain and pound shops often sell salt pots made from tough glass that are safe for children to use. Or you could use plastic squeezy tomatoes meant for ketchup, or plastic sauce bottles to draw and make trails.

Turn it round

Washers, nuts and screws

What you need:

▶ construction sets with screws and bolts
▶ nuts and bolts of all sorts and sizes
▶ bottles and jars with screw tops
▶ keys and locks
▶ doorknobs
▶ boxes with keys
▶ small padlocks and keys

I will need

Contribution to Early Learning Goals:

PRIME	SPECIFIC
Physical Development ①	Expressive arts & design ① ②

What you do:

The twisting action of turning screws, nuts and bolts is a very good exercise for coordination, control and concentration. You can provide this through commercial products or more inventive solutions. Add some of these to your repertoire:

1. Contact local DIY and hardware stores to see if they have any surplus nuts and bolts for free play and exploration. They can be any size, and a variety is good. Children will sometimes play for long periods, removing and replacing the nuts on the right bolts.

2. Get some thin strips of wood and drill small holes in these so children can fix them together with nuts and bolts.

3. Old fashioned analogue clocks with lots of parts are getting more rare, but parents and carers may be able to donate old clocks. You can then provide small screwdrivers for exploring the mechanisms of these machines, by taking them apart.

4. Easy fix kits such as Gears and Knex, leading to plastic and metal Meccano sets, Constructor, Brio Builder and Erector are useful staples, and these can be mixed for variety and interest.

5. Make a collection of screw-topped plastic bottles and jars. Remove the tops and challenge the children to find the right tops for the containers.

6. Make a storage unit for small items such as collage bits by screwing plastic pots with screw tops to a piece of wood so children need to take off the screw tops to get the things they need.

7. Collect boxes, cases and bags with locks and keys. Collect the little padlocks from suitcases and put them all in a box with the keys.

And another idea:

▶ Buy a wooden screw toy (the Wood Multi-construction Kit), suitable for younger children, from Letterbox **www.letterbox.co.uk**

▶ Get some wind-up toys and cars for wrist and finger turning.

Bash it!

Hammering

What you need:

- soft wood offcuts
- driftwood, balsa wood
- small woodworking tools
- children's workbench
- nails, screws
- wood glue and clamps to hold wood in place
- suitable storage and organisation for tools

Contribution to Early Learning Goals:

PRIME	SPECIFIC
Physical Development ①	Expressive arts & design ① ②

What you do:

Woodwork with real tools is a challenge, but more and more settings are making this activity available to children in the EYFS. Of course you need to attend to safety issues, and supervision is essential, particularly as children get used to the tools and equipment, but where woodwork is available the effect on confidence, concentration and hand-eye coordination is significant. Find out where woodwork is offered in local settings and go and see it in action, or consult your Local Authority for guidance on Woodwork in the EYFS. Here are some simple ideas you could try:

1. Younger children can get used to hammering by using hammering toys, but hammering nails into a big log or tree stump which won't move is much more fun!

2. You could start by offering sandpaper and wood glue for sticking offcuts together. Driftwood is softer than wood from shops, or ask DIY shops and local carpenters for offcuts.

3. Locate a supplier of real, small-sized tools. Toy tools are frustrating and cheap tools can be dangerous.

4. As children get more used to woodwork you can add small hand saws, brace and bit drills, simple planes and screwdrivers.

5. Storage and care of woodworking materials is crucial. It's a good idea to start with a shadow board for tools, so children know where to put them, and teach safe use of each tool as you introduce it.

6. You could ask parents if one of them would be willing to come to your setting to help with woodwork, to provide adult presence and a good model. Or ask a local carpenter to come and demonstrate what he does, bringing his tools, talking about how to be safe, and demonstrating some simple processes.

And another idea:

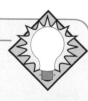

▶ 'Be Safe' is a booklet on safety in schools is published by ASE (The Association for Science Education) and contains information on safety in schools.

▶ Brio make a Wooden Builder Set with tools and other kit.

Resources and further information

Books and leaflets

The Little Book of Sewing and Weaving
The Little Book of Nursery Rhymes
The Little Book of Dough
The Little Book of Clay and Malleable Materials
all available from **www.acblack.com/featherstone**

Be Safe – a booklet on safety in schools published by ASE (The Association for Science Education) containing information on safety in schools.

Websites

www.kididdles.com www.gameskidsplay.net or **http://childstoryhour.com**
– for hundreds of stories, rhymes and songs with the words.

www.tts-group.co.uk – or other educational suppliers for aiming games, targets, resistance bands and other equipment for physical development.

www.commotionstore.co.uk - for pipettes, syringes, droppers, plastic tubing and magnets.

ww.stjohnsupplies.co.uk – for good value plastic medical tweezers.

www.plantmenow.co.uk   – for brooms, trowels and other garden tools.
www.garden-gear.co.uk
www.qualitygardentools.com

www.mindstretchers.co.uk – for some great weaving resources.

www.montessoriworld.org/Handwork/weave/weaving1.html – for the Montessori weaving pages.

www.spacekraft.co.uk – for sets of ribbon sticks.

wwww.letterbox.co.uk – for a wooden screw toy suitable for younger children (the Wood Multiconstruction Kit).

www.brio.co.uk – Brio make a Wooden Builder Set with tools and other kit. Look online for a catalogue of suppliers.